IGBOS
THE NEXT AGENDA

IGBOS
THE NEXT AGENDA

SEIMP Revolution towards an Industrialised South-East

E.O. GODWINS

IGBOS: The Next Agenda

First Edition © 1993

Revised and Updated. Copyright © 2023 by E.O. Godwins.

Published in Nigeria by:
MILLENIAL BOOKS

Contents

Dedication

————————————————//————————————————

TO

The teeming number of industrious
Igbo Comrades whose moral
strength and courage stirred a
burning desire in me to put this
treatise together,

AND

My biological family,
My base and closest touch with this
Fraternity of fine Nigerians.

Foreword

It was still early in the evening: Samuel had returned from the rubber plantation an hour before. He was once again attacking the bush of cocoa yams growing wild in the children's open toilet cum refuse dump.

Laughing in childish glee, a mischievous Ebo led us to see Sam's cooking pot to prove that Sam actually cooked and ate the inedible cocoyam heads. And that was his food 21 times a week.

Sam was only one of dozens of young Ibo boys and girls who came to our village late in 1970 after the civil war ended. They came with nothing but themselves. Even the tap-knives and buckets they used to tap rubber were bought by the plantation owners, they would pay for these with their earnings as time wore on. They accepted a lot in life that the children of the "Masters" whom they worked for would not accept, not even in a dream.

Their homes had been destroyed during the war; many were orphans. They had nothing to start life with but their bare palms and ...

And a burning determination to succeed, to rise again.

Today, I have a heartfelt and tender attachment to the Samuel's of this great Nation, Nigeria. Where no one would do a job, they did it. They have made more bricks without being given straw. From the debris of Nnewi, Ogidi, and other centres of massive military bombbasting, they have recreated the "Igbo-made" technology, Nigeria's survival pill in today's SAP.

In 1966, they lost their businesses and immovable assets in many parts of the Nation particularly Northern Region. Again and again in several religion-motivated riots, their investments and assets fall victim of looting and arson like a recurring decimal. In the recent political impasse, the security of life and property that followed rumors of possible war seriously disrupted their business life more than any other set of Nigerians.

In all these things, the Okoro man or Igboman has come to earn my respect because of his tenacity to survive. He seems to convert each set back into strengths immediately. It is my privilege to write a foreword to this treatise by my brother, Godwins who has more than his fair share of that courageous spirit of resilience which characterizes that fraternity of Nigerians – the Igbos. He is here sounding a clarion call to all progressive minded Igbos to convert the last weakness or threat to their enterprise drive, into a strength.

Dear reader, this clarion call is so relevant because an industrial east is not only feasible; it is also affordable and is in fact the only permanent hope of unmolestable security for you. I have no doubt in my mind that you have both the money and know-how to achieve that goal. Then with such a firm anchor hold of an industrialized home base, the crusade for a productive Nigeria, for leadership in ECOWAS trade, also for the industrial, economic and political emancipation of Africa will be on course.

I respect the business and academic drive of the Ijebuman; I admire the courage and hardwork of the Hausa merchants. Among all these the Igboman has been in a peculiar position by geography, politics and an accident of history.

There is no place for tribalism in business where pragmatism alone dictates the tune. Pst. E.O. Godwins is proposing the most pragmatic business solution to a peculiar business climate that faces the Igboman.

Give the Igboman an industrial base at home, and he will compete effectively with Japan and China for world commerce and industry. And that will be good for all and sundry in Nigeria.

Finally, dear reader, I am convinced you have the money and talent to create a safe industrialized home base. I completely endorse the suggestion of Pst. Godwins. Get the accountants and other financial experts; to harness your impressive financial strengths together, and an "industrial East" will spring up.

This is my tribute to the unconquered, unconquerable spirit of the Samuel of Nigeria—The Igbos.

Enobabor Idahosa M.O.
UNIBEN, Benin City

IGBOS: The Next Agenda
Obtainable online at: amazon.com, okadabooks.com &
aeeiafrica.org

ONE

WHO IS AN IGBOMAN?

In the heart of the vast African continent lies Nigeria. A country acclaimed internationally to be the African black power owing to her riches in terms of population (being the most populous black nation in the world) economy, unquantifiable natural resources, human resources and military might, just to mention but a few.

Within this great political entity lies the Igbo race in a heterogeneous and complex Nigeria society that has over four hundred tribes with the Igbos forming more than 35% of her total numerical strength of about 200 million people.

Endowed with a lot of resourceful potentials, the Igboman becomes the symbol of true resource base and gains of hard work. He is industrious and can humble himself to undertake even a menial job with the ultimate goal of making a living, unlike his counterparts. He is resolute. This means that he has a defined goal and pursues it conscientiously with a great determination to succeed. He has never been threatened by a humble beginning because he believes that even when his beginning looks small that his latter end shall be greatly increased. He has a great heart. This makes him never to be satisfied with his economic status at any given time. His ambition for greatness through legal and legitimate means makes him famous for healthy rivalries.

All of the above and lots more make him the tap root of African technology in engineering, commerce and industry.

Realizing this fact, that highly perceptive Second Republic Governor of Kwara State in the person of Alhaji Shaaba Lafiagi made a special reference to it while addressing the NUJ's Conference on the importance of Nigerian Unity. In his words:

> "it is pertinent to mention that the entrepreneurship... as well as the technical know how of the Igbos have become the engine of the industrial and economic development of our country" — *Daily Sunray August 27th 1993*

If Nigeria therefore accepts with the entire world to being the giant of black Africa (and this greatness includes her technology) it will not at any rate be an over statement if the man behind the technology becomes pinpointed as the pivot of African technology.

An Israelite?

Several schools of thought have tried to trace the Igboman's ingenuity to Israeli decent hence his attendant idiosyncrasy believed to be sequel to genetic transfer. Historians and archaeologists, through their various researches have established this claim strongly while his chronological and genealogical linage is traced to Gad, the missing tribe of Israel.

The name "Ibo" is believed to be born out of mispronouncing of the word "Hebrew" by the colonial master who owing to the inability to comprehend the Iboman's accent and diction mistook Hebrew for Ibo.

History is there to establish these claims through nostalgic similitudes such as in culture and socio-economic activities.

Underneath are six points that lend credence to the fact that the Iboman is a natural Israelite. They are:

Culture of No King Except God

In the original plan of God, the Jewish nation was not to have a monarchical institution. A situation which was prevalent for centuries. This was because God himself decided to be their King while they become his people.

Sequel to much pressure from them for a physical King like the gentiles living around them, God obliged them and out of a permissive will established for them a monarchy, an institution which in no distant time met its waterloo. This monarchical issue was an exception and not a rule for any Israelite and so, emphatically therefore, one can state that the Israelites had no King except God.

Similarly, the Iboman does not believe in a physical monarchy. The existence of Kingship in Igbo land today was born out of the colonial master's selfish whim to establish a warrant chieftaincy to enable him authenticate an effective exploitation drive after being greeted with disappointments in the Eastern part of the country; a situation which was opposed to the traditional monarchy existing in the other tribes of Nigeria.

Culture of Circumcision

God gave the Israelites a law to circumcise their male children on the eighth day starting from the date of birth for by so doing, a covenant of sonship was established. This has been dominant among the Igbo's right from the stone age. A culture which looked strange to some other tribes that if not for the intervention of the World Health Organization through whose enlightenment campaigns, most tribes followed suit, the reverse should have been the case. Funny enough, up to date, some tribes still don't practice it.

Monogamy

In Nigeria, while other tribes see polygamy as one of the signs for greatness and as successful achievement, the Igboman on the contrary holds strongly to monogamy as a way of life even when he is not holding strongly to Christian religious ideals. Moreso where there are exceptional cases they are in the negligible minority. That is to show that it is not the rule.

Does this not tally with the Lord's mandate to the Jews to refrain from polygamy which made that culture illegal?

Monotheism

God passed a law to the Jews and told them saying "Thou shall have no other gods before me, of the likeness of anything either in heaven or on the earth or beneath the earth. Don't bow down unto them nor worship them" Based on this, it becomes a culture that the God of heaven alone be worshipped in Israel.

Despite the usual universal moral aberration and spiritual lethargy which have derailed some, the average Igboman is still known for his religious ideals and devotion to all shades of Christian denominations. This establishes his faith in that divine blue print. It is almost a taboo to own an idol or a shrine in Igbo land. Even those who do so, do it in hiding. This is not true of some other tribes in Nigeria where idol worship is still as popular as it was in the stone ages.

In Festivals

The Jewish Nation has a custom that mandates her to offer the first fruit of her increase during harvest to God.

In like manner, the Iboman holds strongly to the New yam festival custom which advocates his paying tribute to a higher authority (God) with a percentage of his harvest annually. A custom which predates history and from every dimension agrees with that of the Jews.

In Technology

After the scramble for Jerusalem in A.D. 70, the Jews who scattered all over the face of the earth turned out to become scientific geniuses who through their technical know-how researched the world into scientific and technological break throughs. Today, it is no exaggeration to state that the brain behind American, Russian, British and even German technology is the Jew. In a nutshell, no Jew, no technology.

Similarly, the Igboman in his socio-economic life has displayed such ingenuity that his technical know-how in technology, commerce and industry makes him an unbeatable rival. A situation that tallies with that of the Jews. In substance, these similitudes lend very strong credence to the claim that the Igbo man is a Jew.

TWO

Industrial Awakening and How It All Began

In Africa, it is noted that the key economic activity of the average man revolved around agriculture. This was enhanced by endowment of nature in areas such as favourable tropics, vegetation and land mass. It also connotes a very low level of technology which made him depend on the industrialized nations of the world for technical goods and services while his agricultural products became his mainstay for balance of payments when exported.

This situation held sway in Nigeria with the Eastern Region being predominantly responsible for palm produce as cash crop in the absence of other edibles, the West majoring on cocoa, the Mid-west on timber and rubber, while the North dwelt on livestock, cotton, hides and skins, and groundnuts.

While this was on course, the Igbos (who unlike her Western and Northern counterparts that had enough land resources and forest reserves), were faced with restriction to expansion in agriculture. This was owing to her population density which could be estimated to run about an average of a thousand settlers per square kilometer in her usual farm settlement system of living.

Though we are not talking history, it will interest you to note that the scramble for farmlands which made the Igboman evolve the farm settlement system of living ended up almost erasing the idea of forest reserves in the East.

With this non-availability of sufficient land, the hardworking Igboman became incapacitated from delving into commercial agriculture and as a result, tended towards commerce as a second career while his farm remained for subsistence.

From this, we find that the cradle of Igbo technology was her choice of commerce as a second career. This is boosted by a natural endowment on her race with a great wealth of highly intelligent manpower coupled with a healthy rivalry instigated by encouraging challenges.

On the second rung of the ladder are the challenges of the man-made difficulties posed before the Igbos in the form of economic blockade during the civil war when they were forced into total isolation from the outside world and as a result were compelled to either evolve their own technology, produce their food and services or die in isolation. This intended strangulation ended up working out for their good as they took their destinies in their hands by facing the challenges squarely.

Though a child as at then, I can still remember a lot about the Biafran made battery, hand grenades, 'ogbunigwe' explosive, shore battery (sea mines) mechanical fabrications, detergents, and crude oil refining etc. In a nutshell, almost every essential technical commodity of the Western world ended up having a Biafran alternative.

A situation which was not outlived by the over-running of the Biafran republic.

Once a child is born, the next thing expected of him is growth. This is because, as simple biology teaches, one of the characteristics that differentiates an animate object from the inanimate one is life. That life is expressed in growth. Same is the case with the Igboman's War instigated technology.

When the civil war ended, the Igboman was smart enough to know that he had slim chances of being reabsorbed into the public service and the army, coupled with fear of the Victor/Vanquished syndrome. So, through courage and an indomitable mental attitude, he refused to succumb to a predicament of becoming down-trodden by a clean switch-over to self-employment. This maiden decision led to a rise in his self-confidence and he soon started to re-experiment with his war-taught discoveries. Thus, like today's industrial and technological giant of the world, Japan that sprang up from a nuclear blast ashes of Hiroshima and Nagasaki, the Igboman's efforts gave birth eventually to our crafts and technology of today. Internationally, it is noted that war affected cities or countries hardly survive the adverse effects of war aftermaths. Such cases abound today in Hiroshima, Iraq, Karwait, etc.

The Eastern States of Nigeria were battered and ravaged by the concerted assault of the Federal Military dingdong during the thirty-month civil war. The region was left a desolation that suggested no economic promise whatever: a terribly ruined region. Hence the whole world is baffled today at the speed with which the economic reconstruction was achieved through self-help.

The Igboman's hard work and know-how did not only give rise to a speedy reconstruction but also introduced industrial awakening, rural development, self-reliance and architecture. A visit to Eastern Nigeria will confirm it. The rate at which privately owned industries sprang up since after the war is so astonishing that the former Head of State, President Ịbrahim Babangida, after visiting the Aba International trade fair in 1989 confessed that owing to what he saw, (technological and industrial break-through in the East) not even the Federal industries could compete favourably with the private sector over there. Of course, this made him to consider Abia State for the Nigerian Industrial Research Centre as at then.

Eastern industrial proliferation has escalated to the extent of having almost all the local government head-quarters saturated. To crown it all, Nigeria's one and half decades of economic recession which led to the introduc-tion of economic measures like SAP finally gave a cata-pulted blow-up to these war generated small-scale firms turning those manual workshops into the multi-national companies of today with stocks quoted at the stock exchange market. An example of such companies is

PRODA at Enugu which is the first indigenous company to manufacture a vehicle by using about eighty percent of local raw materials for its fabrication.

Home Consciousness

The civil war left a big scar on the Igboman. As an enterprising man that settled in every nook and cranny of the nation, he lost all his personal assets at the outbreak of National hostilities against him in 1966. Back home, while hiding in his ancestral village from an enemy with superior fire power, lack of accommodation, food and other amenities created epidemic conditions that killed most members of his upper class citizens much faster that the enemy could kill. Owing to his painful memory, the Igboman has established a code of "NO Jerusalem, no uttermost part of the world" (or simply put; "home consciousness") immediately after the civil war. A healthy situation which contrasts sharply, the pre-war mentality of urban concentration.

Rural Urbanisation and Conurbation

One other thing that the Igboman learnt from the civil war was that he is the architect of his fortune or misfortune. That means that he could through hard work recover all that he has lost. This realization made him depend less on Government for anything.

By this order, his post war rural housing scheme which competes favourably with urban planned housing projects, along with his communal efforts in procuring public utilities such as potable water, post offices, road network, electricity, schools and other infrastructural facilities made rural urbanization in the East second to none elsewhere.

The rural development being on course coupled with towns conurbating with and annexing their neighbours in the presence of the afore-mentioned provision for infrastructural facilities, the Eastern "rurals" without mincing words have provided for a healthy industrial climate.

THREE

THE CALL

Migration

Migration is an essential characteristic of viable labour; skilled labour must of necessity be mobile. This is caused either by submission to invincible pressures mounted by those who need one's services or a quest for greener pastures and more favourable climates. As a result, the Igboman has been noted to be the greatest migrant in Africa. In fact, he is in every nation of the world.

He migrates to use his skills to exploit untapped opportunities and thereby contributes his quota to the development of his host society. He is often an economic catalyst, enhancing industrialization and housing projects. This is how over 60% of Igbos happen to be emigrants to various parts of the World.

There is nothing wrong with this. The Igboman leaves home, exploits potentials and untapped opportunities and he generates capital enough to embark on industrial establishments. And there the problem begins. Our problem is with cohesion and co-ordination of these production capabilities acquired through hardwork and creativity; often building one's capital up from absolutely nothing. How do we utilize these hard-won gains?

Unsafe Business Bases

Today, the amount of trading capital in the hands of Igbos is truly impressive. In every field where Nigerians have to depend on their own strength, creativity and toughness to survive, the Igboman is champion – Mechanics, Fabrication, distributive trade, hand crafts; they are there. Hence one can safely say they constitute the engine of Nigerian Commerce and Industry. They developed these trades from nothing, often far away from home, in their host communities.

They grow big and invest millions in their business bases in their host societies. All is well until the day of National upheaval. Like January to June 1966.

Suddenly, the Igbos are killed and butchered and their assets looted. The survivors flee home, and loose everything! The business bases they built into billions of Naira from nothing:

Again, from nothing, the tough Igboman builds up a big business base worth billions. Again, one religious upheaval after the other comes and his business goes up in smoke.

Last time, with uncertainties over the June 12 related political imbroglio in 1993–94, more than anyone else, the business of the Igboman was disrupted as he scurried home to the East. Hundreds of thousands of Naira was spent packing home and later packing back. Often, tears stung my eyes as I watched the ordeal. O the innocent lives lost in the countless accidents that occurred as a result! The pains and agony: even the schooling of children was disrupted. Business? It fell to pieces: Only years to come will quantify the losses in revenue that resulted.

It is all the more painful because there need not have been so much loss. We are yet to learn one small lesson since 1966. That lesson is that the most important concern to anyone investing in high capital base business is SAFETY.

In today's Nigeria, every political and scientific indices, or indicators have shown that the country called Nigeria is a mere geographical expression that will never know peace until the fundamental issues of marginalization, discrimination, unhealthy supremacy contest which cause nepotism, tribalism, ethnicity and political imbalance are addressed through a deliberate/constitutional restructuring of this country.

As far as this remains a day dream, Nigeria will remain a fragile clay pot bereft of national unity and peace which are the principal factors required for the siting of a business and (or) an industry.

Insecurity and lack of safety of the life and business of the Igboman, have become a daily occurrence even in Nigeria, his own country. Whenever there is any political, social or economic imbrogho, Igbo man becomes the scape goat for venting accumulated venom and vendetta that are seemingly propelled by jealousy.

Let us do an inquest of 2023 presidential election for instance. With the constitutional right of every Nigerian Citizen to either vote, or be voted for into any elective office in Nigeria, the Igboman has been projected by words and action as one who does not deserve any elective ambition to the highest political office in Nigeria since after the civil war. He is even disenfranchised to say the least, but this time, against all odds and by divine election, Peter Obi who is an Igbo Politician indicated his interest to contest for Presidency. For this ambition, the ruling party's presidential candidate and some of his foot soldiers changed from the democratic practice of soliciting for votes to win an election to anti-igbo campaign of calumny through which incitement, many Igbos lost their lives and businesses as they were being attacked with impunity and without defense.

What offence did the Igbos commit to deserve this treatment? The offence is that they voted for Peter Obi of Labour Party. In the history of Nigerian democracy, the Igbo has demonstrated that he is the most detribalized Nigerian. The Igbo is known to have voted en-bloc to bring about the victory of Chief MKO Abiola in 1993 despite having an Igbo Vice Presidential candidate to NPN's Tofa of Kano.

In 1999, Igbos gave President Olusegun Obasanjo their block votes in his two terms elections in spite of having the highly Igbo-respected Dim Chukwuemeka Odumegwu Ojukwu as a vigorous contender for presidency at the same time.

In similar vein, Igbos gave same block votes to President Umaru Musa Yar'Adua in 2007. They did same for President Goodluck Jonathan in his 2011 Presidential election for which Gen Mohammadu Buhari of CPC challenged the credibility of over 6 million votes from South East for Jonathan.

Also, in Jonathan's re-election bid in 2015, the Igbos repeated the same history of block-voting Jonathan. Finally, 2019, the Igbos gave H.E. Atiku Abubakar block votes.

In all these, Igbos were not asked to leave Lagos, or tagged "tribal voters". They were "good" Nigerians who remain tolerated as far as they continue to eke out a living doing their legitimate artisan works and trading, but never to think becoming Nigeria's President.

Igbos voted for Mr. Peter Obi, not because of his tribe but because of his competence. He was never the first Igbo man to contest for this position since 1960. Not even Dr. Nnamdi Azikiwe got the support of Nigerians, and the Igbos like Peter Obi. He is a Nigerian Project, and not an Igbo Project, but the overzealous tribal politicians made an antidemocratic narrative of tribal politics out of the good wishes of Nigerian electorate for which they intend to make political gain at the detriment of Igboman's life and investment in Lagos, using their popular "Igbo must go" slogan.

It is now time for the Igboman to learn his bitter lesson from this ugly outcome. They tell us to our bare faces that we don't have rights to protect. Why do they say so? They say so because you have all your businesses, properties, investments, etc. in their community. They know very well that you cannot even try to fight for any rights since you have a lot to lose as ransom as it concerns your assets in your host communities nationwide.

They will do this with bold face because you are the only tribe that will develop your host community and keep your own land only for burying your dead that can only be ferried down at death for burial. But when it comes to making meaningful developments through investments, you concentrate everything in your host communities.

If I may ask you; how many none Igbos have companies, factories, schools and landed properties in any of the South East States? This is why they will wear bold face when undoing us because there will surely be no retribution as they have nothing in your territory to lose.

While the monolith north constantly threatens to confiscate our 44 Trillion dollars assets and investments if we dare talk of being given a chance to be free Nigerians, the West threatens and matches their own threat with equivalent action by burning our markets, revoking and demolishing our properties rights with reckless abandon.

They tell us to our face to go back to the East and leave Lagos for them. In order to frustrate you out, they slam you with multiple taxation like the Egyptian task Masters.

In view of all these antics, the Igbo is put in a cage with clipped feathers not to protest against human right violation expressed in local colonialism, imperialism and exploitation by his fellow citizens.

He always keeps mum calculating what he stands to lose if he wants to make his voice heard by demanding for his fair share. The Igboman is not qualified to rule Nigeria, neither is he qualified to man the main stream economic hubs in the oil and gas sector, the NNPC, NPA or to head the Armed Forces, the Police, Parastatal and juicy Ministries in Federal Executive arm of government.

The Igbo man is out there with his business littered in every place because the Federal government refused to give us our due share of infrastructure such as sea port, international airports (until recently) railway, good roads, and industries. Since this is the case, we have to go and develop the East by ourselves and play safe. We shall stop forcing one Nigeria spirit (which we believe and practice by developing our host communities all over the country) on unrepentant tribal and ethnic jingoists and bigots. The unity of Nigeria has always been at the expense of Igbo Man's blood. Enough is enough.

A Safe Anchor Base

Our first law of success should be "Invest where and when your life and property are safest". This is perhaps what that illustrious son of Igboland underscored; His Excellency, Governor Chukwuemeka Ezeife when he launched the "Think Home: Consciousness" at NICON NUGA HILTON ABUJA during his tenure.

In attendance were most of the famous industrialists and merchants of Anambra State. And at the end of that symposium, the government of Anambra State provided a "Think Home" Industrial Estate which is currently serving the people.

The point being made is that Igbos, all over the World should think and consider home when they establish high capital base enterprises. Invest in a safe soil.

The safe soil we all know is back home in the East. We recognize this, that is why we all run there in times of national trouble. The only anchor base that will make our business impregnable to malicious attacks is an INDUSTRIALIZED EAST

The JAPANESE are a war vanquished people: but they are masters of the world economy today because they have brains; the enterprising spirit and an industrialized home. (Their home is even a volcanic Island). We are in every respect constrained as Japan is; we are better endowed than them. Our survival must be an Industrial East.

The Clarion Call

Our homeland, because that is where we feel safest, is today reserved for the day we come in tears. What father will love children who come home only when they are in trouble? When they celebrate, do good things or acquire honour, they do it outside?

It is good that the Igboman has face-lifted his every village (from Abriba to Mgbidi, Ohafia to Ngwo) into a modern township with all infrastructure. But that is not good enough! Because at best, we come there for only a few days to consume the savings of a whole year at Christmas and run back.

The solution to this is to make our every business have roots at home and that looks like a very tall order. How can the electronics merchant, whose customers are in Kaduna and Lagos come and do his business at home? He cannot. But there is something he can do and that is the Clarion Call I sound—the whole reason I am writing this treatise.

Every worthy Igboman must begin to invest additional funds he generates from his trade into industrial and technical undertakings that are based in the East—Your Safe Haven. It could be Shoe-Works, animal farms, meat processing plants, Garment factories, tools and fabrication factories etc. Cooperatives, joint ventures and joint stock or Ltd Liability Companies are cases to consider.

What I am saying is not new to any of us. Many of us probably generated our first capital by hawking newspapers; then the funds generated were used to open a bookshop. The bookshop now generated enough money to open a big printing press which is located far away from home and hence, during times of National Upheaval, this Printing Press is target of envious and malicious attacks. I am saying take one step further: Use this printing press to generate funds to start a gigantic Publishing House based in the East that can serve your customers all over the nation and worldwide. If your money is not enough to do so don't wait; enter a joint Venture or partnership or even joint stock with others to start it. The call is "Start now".

This is the only way to be safe and unassailable. Get an industrialized home base. Then if the place you are operating becomes unsafe, you can close shop and run home. Hunger or lack of business will not drive you out!

Japan has its customers all over the world, including Nigeria. But they don't have to come here to do business. Their industrial factories based in Japan service all their customers worldwide and they make their millions daily, quietly.

We must likewise develop an industrial East in this Country. Then all our present distributive trades and other commercial undertakings, can be run in conjunction with sons of the soil while we concentrate on industrial factory productions and related services in the East. Then alone can we talk meaningfully of lasting National Unity.

Learning from Past Mistakes of Others

It is a known fact that indigenes (Sons of the Soil) don't like hardworking strangers especially when they are subservient under-boys. But hard work leads to success and success breads jealousy. Jealousy of less successful sons of the soil. Man is imperfect after all.

In many places he has been to, the enterprising Igboman has been a victim of this jealousy. Indigenes becoming jealous, not of his hard work, but of his success! How do you expect to make one Million Naira in another man's land when he has not been able to make even Ten thousand and you expect he won't raise an eye brow in protest? Even Abraham in the Bible suffered this fate. The sons of the soil, (the Canaanites) gave him barren and arid lands to live in. But in the height of an absolute drought in the whole area, Abraham had water in his wells in his own part of the land. Of course, the indigenes drove him out of the land: Capital Jealously.

This kind of Jealousy has been demonstrated against the Igbos again and again in lootings and killings during moments of ill-motivated National or regional Upheaval.

Such was the case with the ferocious 1966 hostilities against the Igboman. One day the son of the soil was laughing with him, drinking his beer and being nice neighbour. The following day, he turned against the Igboman with great slaughter and looting. It was so ferocious that it was out of proportion with any purported immediate cause. It was jealousy pent-up like a smouldering fire for so long, and let loose at the least opportunity. That is what was the remote cause and the thing at the bottom of that magnitude of hostilities.

In religious riots, one after the other the story has been repeated. Lootings, maimings and killings.

Since the past 30years, and still counting, the cases of Matasine riots, insurgency, Boko Haram, ISWAP, and other crisis with rumours of war and chaos, the Igboman suffered. Who blames him for running? He has been bitten more than twice. Why shouldn't he be shy for once? Fear of repeating pains of the past is very real and tangible. But how many senseless deaths in accidents during the stampede home and packing back!

Now is the time to find a permanent solution – an Industrial East. Time will fail me to remind you of those whose properties were seized in the early '70s in Ghana and Equatorial Guinea! Is it losses during threat of expulsion from Camerouns; the properties seized by Charles Taylor in Liberia earlier in their political turmoil of the '90s? The wealth and assets of Nigerians seized recently by Gabonese. What of the South African xenophobic attacks on Nigerians? Why over-flog the thing; I am sure you know what I am talking about.

The Stage is Set at Home: Utilise it

In every nook and cranny of the East, small villages have been transformed into modern townships with all modern amenities: water, light, medical centers, postal services and roads among others. Most of these were through the personal efforts of the Igboman, not government. Housing is standard and adequate: standards of housing other tribes build only in their State Capitals are to be found dotted in small villages in the East. Many of these rural communities also have the essential telephone service.

The stage is set. The atmosphere is just ripe for small scale industrial factories to take off! Let's learn even from China that exported matches, handkerchiefs, pocket mirrors, pencils and small factory made ceramic for many years. These generated the funds that built their Nuclear technology of today!

Start now, we would soon be masters of African Commerce and Industry if we do. But who will strike the first blow in the bid for a long-dreamed industrial Revolution? You of course!

Cost of Alien Status

Today, Igbos are being used. Communities, Local Governments and even states use them to enhance development in ways verging on exploitation.

Recently, a local authority in one State planned an Urban Scheme and resettled a set of mainly Igbo traders in an uninhabited Suburb of the metropolis. They had to use their hard-earned capital to build a magnificent market to continue trading and survive! Surprisingly, the local government did not reimburse the cost of building as promised; yet keeps harassing the poor "aliens" for revenue collection.

Even areas the indigenes consider as forbidden due to Superstition, are given to Igbos. They open them up and the sons of the soil take-over. Experimental Guinea Pigs?

A state-owned Ultra-modern Market is opened one place or the other. The Champion of the distributive trade is the Igboman. But the sons of the Soil get all the Stalls for ₦50,000 P.A. They sub-let to the Igboman at prices ranging from ₦750,000 P.A. to an outrageous ₦1,500,000.00 P.A. He has to take it if he must survive.

Hence, we enhance development at great personal costs in other people's lands while our own remains desolate. We are not home except for about four days during Christmas and other festivals; or when we come in tears during times of national crises.

Enough is enough. The time has come when our own home too must be developed to boom all year round with industrial factory life.

The Race Has Started: Join Now

Let me end this section by citing the praise worthy example of that Strongman of Urualla, the Chairman of FERDINAND GROUP. He had well decentralized establishments all over Nigeria and overseas, but at some point made an Eastern drift. He located the corporate Headquarters of his Companies in his ancestral town, Urualla. In addition, he established seven other multimillion Naira industries which are managed today by skilled expatriates. This is an excellent example of a man utilizing the favorable rural industrial climate. And of course, the investment base is safe at all times and in all events. Of course, he received a notable award for this achievement.

Start today: channel your investible funds into industrial undertakings based at home.

THE PROMISE

It is true the peculiar position that the Igboman occupies in the scheme of things in Nigeria is enviable. He has been so placed, that for bare survival, he must take the courses of action he has been taking. The call for an industrial home base is one step further in this process. Once this is done, how enviable his position is will become truly obvious.

To safeguard assets, the Igboman must consider as a matter of urgency, an Eastern movement. The natural and automatic result of this will be industrial concentration with all its attendant opportunities for development and progress in technology. Avenues for manpower development will increase, and this is a zone already rich in highly creative human resources. Added to this is the fact that most infrastructural facilities already exist. The 'Eastern region' can become the Japan of Africa by A.D. 2033.

The boost of SAP and other economic reconstruction measures are very real and tangible too. One of the primary goals of these programmes is self-reliance and self-sufficiency. So, small scale industries are protected. SAP has made us to look inwards for sourcing our materials locally. Exploiting the opportunity of this period has led to growth explosion in many of our young industries even now.

A visit to Aba and Nnewi will confirm this. These are now Industrial Cities where mere cobbling workshops, sewing houses, and even fabricating and welding workshops have "blown-up" into multi-million Naira shoe factories, Garment Industries and Engineering tools/ Equipment Companies. Almost all banned goods of Western Origin now have their Nigerian alternative, thanks to the popular "Igbo-made", courtesy of SAP.

Complete Industrialization by A.D. 2033 is possible and very much within our reach. All we need is summon the courage to consummate this industrial pioneering.

What follows are my suggestions on how you and I can participate in, and have a portion of, the gains of this march. I may not succeed in keeping out technical and financial terms as much as I have done to this point. I can only promise that it should be easily understandable.

The Three Tier Production Chain and Logistics

Business is concerned with organizing production. Simply, put goods and services needed by the people together and production is enhanced. To produce a bar of Soap is a factory, technical job. To ware-house and distribute this soap is a commercial service, as well as transportation and finance. The soap does not get to the hands of consumers until it has passed through the retail shop owner's hands.

The above, in a perhaps simplistic model, outlines the three tiers of the production chain: primary production (make the soap), Distribution cum warehousing (2nd tier) and retailing (3rd tier). All these require different techniques of management and involve different kinds of businessmen/women.

The only reason each of us invests our time and money in anything, say soap production, is because there is market. We sell and get our money back plus some profit. That means without market, there can be no business. Hence the final focus is on the consumer wherever he/she may be; which has often necessitated our settling down to operate our businesses where we find our markets.

But the need for safety and security is a senior economic concern that must be considered before the consideration of an existing market for our business. That is why no one invests in a country experiencing a raging war.

The whole essence of this treatise is that our peculiar experience demands that we establish a base for our businesses at home.

What I recommend here is that the first tier of our production (technology based mass production in factories e.g. soap-making) must be based at home in the East. Other distributors and sub-distributors can be satellited throughout the rest of the Country or even the entire world. Retailing can then remain the vital link with the market.

This process that will get production from a safe Industrial East to reach your present Customers/market, where ever they may be is commercial logistics. The man who manufactures is not the man who distributes and the man who distributes is not the one who retails. The manufacturer should be home based while retailers operate outside where the customers are.

Learning from Others

We have examples to learn from in this path to Industrialization. We shall consider only Israel and Japan here.

Israel as a nation was gathered from over one hundred and forty nations worldwide. There are always complications associated with this kind of change of environment; but we agree that no sacrifice is too great to pay to protect the future of unborn generations. Today, Israel has built a formidable economy.

Japan was a nation whose economy was ruined by war-inflicted man-made hazards after the Second World War this made her a dumping ground for products of the International business community. Their famous economic miracle was not without a sacrificial stage like the one we face today. I can still remember that after the World War II ended in 1945, the first measure taken by the Japanese government was a campaign for home consciousness. These stances made international migration (and financial deployment) seem a cultural taboo. Leaving the Islands of Honshu, Hokaido, Shikokhu and Khushu earned a Japanese serious disdain, ostracization and stigmatization.

Thus, the Japanese nation had a proper accountability for, and proper utilization of, her human resources. It banished the ills of brain drain. The most valuable asset of any nation is its nationals – its people.

Today, all routes lead to a highly industrialized Japan in triumph over all her natural and unnatural (man-made) Constraints. And we are in every way constrained; in every way endowed as they were.

The eastern states are rich for producing us: only that our wealth has rubbed off more on other places commerce wise, than our home. By proper management of our human resources, we can colonize the World's technology of today!

Only let us learn from the mistakes of our fathers. Posterity and future generations of our children yet unborn will not forgive us if we don't. Let us learn from peoples who have translated threats like the ones we face into industrial strengths; and the whole of Nigeria will be glad we did.

Dynamics of Finance

When a man fills a cup from a drum of oil, the oil will soon be finished, it is consumption. But when a bigger drum is being filled from a small cup of oil, there will soon be surplus; it is savings/investment. The enigmatic world of finance!

To finance this industrial drift need not rely on a multi-billion-dollar world bank loan to finance a National Steel company or Petrochemical complex. When you use $10b to finance a company (management) that has never generated $10m, you are drawing a cup of oil from the Drum; it is consumption. You produce looting and corruption. Nigeria's 63years of squander proves that! Neither Steel nor Petrochemical Complex has helped Nigeria. Instead, they are sick babies on which more public funds are spent yearly. Needless to mention that you and I have no share or portion in that spending.

Again and again, we have filled drums of oil from our little cup. A man taps rubber to raise some money and becomes a rubber merchant. From the proceeds of the trade, he starts a rubber factory; that is progress. A newspaper Vendor gets enough money to start a bookshop. Then he makes enough money from the bookshop to start a publishing House. That is growth. And we do this every day. The technical aspects I will point out below are mere extensions of this familiar principle.

In finance, it is not how much money you have that is important but how much income (additional money from sales) that you can generate. If a man with ₦10,000.00 earns ₦1,000.00 a week) he is no match for the man with only ₦2,000.00 to hawk creams and soap who makes ₦400.00 only per week. Give them only 5years; the ₦2,000.00 hawker will be a bigger business man if he keeps the hard work. He is making ₦2.00 on every ₦10.00 while the other one is making only ₦1.00 on every ₦10.00

You may have only ₦2,000.00 or two million naira to trade with today and you think the people that should think of industrial East are the people with ten million Naira trading in big engineering items and electronics. Wrong.

If you must use sales from palm oil trade to build a Palm oil milling factory, you must plan towards it. You save your sales, utilize it in the most gainful way because you have a goal in mind. Then one day, you achieve it. That is how we all got where we are now. This is what Accountants refer to when they talk of sinking funds and capital Redemption Reserve Management.

One other area we scarcely recognize but that will help in financing this industrial goal, is "Financial leverage". A lever is a long rod you use to move a bigger load than your own hands can carry—like what mini bus drivers who cannot buy jack call Babangida Jack: that is a long plank on a ream of tyre that they use to "Jack" their buses.

The lever to jack your funds to finance a big industry is credit (using other people's money to make your profits). Your past performance to make ₦2.00 on every ₦10.00 every week (₦104.00 profit from trading with ₦10.00 in a year!) gives your customers, your suppliers and your bank confidence in you that you can also make more in future. The supplier will give you more goods because he knows you can pay after selling. The customer is ready to pay in advance because he knows that you are to supply. This money is not your own but you have it to use and make yourself bigger profits, than your money can make! You have levered your profits.

Your bankers also know when you have achieved this level of performance. Just like the buyer and seller that let you trade with their money, the bank will grant you loans if you show accounts for such past performance and plans on how to use the money you request to trade successfully in the future. This is where loan proposals and feasibility studies come in. There are many Accountants and economists in our midst who can help you with these.

Let me assert here that there is a limit your own funds and profits can carry you. Industrial establishment is not done anywhere in the world without the power of credit.

Once you enter industrial production stage, you can easily attract international trade partners and capture foreign funds to expand the same way you captured local credit.

From here on you employ and enjoy the intricate dynamics of inter-regional and international finance.

The point being made about dynamics of fiancé is simple. When you traded with ₦5,000.00 in a small chemist with the mind of growing enough to own a production Pharmacy, you planned towards it and achieved it. By employing the dynamics of financial growth outlined above, you can much more easily own an industrial factory. Only dare to aspire and plan for it.

Another source of finance to consider is sale of Goodwill. I will explain this. The Bookshop business you have built up from nothing now has customers and can make profits of up to ₦100,000.00 every year. All that future profit/business belongs to you. You can sell it by selling the business. If all properties or stock of the Bookshop (Books, counters etc.) is ₦25,000.00, buyers are often willing to pay both the ₦25,000.00 as well as an extra may be ₦50,000.00 for the chance to own all the future annual profits of ₦100,000.00 every year. The extra ₦50,000.00 is Goodwill. You can sell 4 bookshops or electronics shops to start a factory!

Technical Support Services

To achieve the stage of growth called for here, some essential services must be employed. Happily enough we have them.

(a) *Track Records and Accounts:* Both for purposes of raising loans and greater management control, a lot more financial records and controls than we now use must be employed. Japan's industries cannot dare to operate without these accounting and financial services. We can't either. If you generate more than ₦10,000.00 profits a month, get people who know how to, let them set up a simple Accounting system to record and control your business for you. You cannot move much further and as fast as you ought to in this drive for Industrial foothold if you don't.

(b) *Management consultancy and Management Audits:* A Clerk earning ₦40,000 a month can keep all the accounts for your ₦500,000 monthly profit; with these records and accounts, consultancy firms can work with you on expert management of your finances and your business. Today a man maybe making ₦4.00 a month on every ₦10.00 when he was trading with ₦5,000.00. That is ₦2, 000.00 as profits monthly. It is not unusual when the same person begins to make ₦1.00 a month on each ₦10.00, when he is already trading with ₦5,000.00 i.e. ₦50,000.00 monthly profit. The ready excuse is that he can no longer pay personal attention to details because it is too big now. With proper use of management consulting to provide management expertise for the growth, this cannot be. You are supposed to reap more profits due to economies of scale.

(c) *Engineering and Technical Consultancy:* During the SAP of the early 1990's, tablets of soap that used to cost ₦1.00 for 4 became one for ₦10.00 to ₦15.00.

Today, thanks to Igbo-made, we have locally manufactured alternatives that cost half as much. But when I get into a processing shop where this soap is made, it pains me to see how much cost and labor are spent on cutting up the soap into tablets of the required size!

By consulting our fabrication experts and engineers, simple machines can be made that can cut the soaps much more neatly and at far less cost than the cost of labor paid now. Not to talk of some inferior chemical properties of the soap which simple chemical engineering consultancy can improve and make the soap of higher quality. This in turn will increase sales and profits. The same applies to virtually all other trades. Let's learn to employ engineering, other technical and financial planning services. We can so easily afford them; we lose so much money because we don't.

Micro-Economic Management (Inter-Firm)

The act of running your own business is micro-economic management. You can extend this use of your own funds to include using the funds of another person's business for mutual benefit or what we may call inter-firm maneuver. I explain.

More heads are better than one. The load that one rope cannot support, if two ropes are twined together, they can support it. So too, a factory that the funds of your business cannot finance, if you join hands with the owner of another business like your own, you can finance it and share profits. For example, two very skilled shoe makers may be making shoes and bags in their respective work places in Lagos and Ibadan. But neither of them can finance the machines to establish a shoe factory in Aba. But through these inter-firm maneuvers, the two can pool their moneys together to build the factory that can supply better shoes and bags to all their customers in Lagos and Ibadan. This can be done in one or a number of ways.

One way of doing this is partnership. The two write an agreement on how much money each will contribute; how to manage the factory and how they will share profits. This is called a deed of partnership. Another way is joint venture. In this method, the factory operates as if they are not running it jointly as partners; but the factory is owing each person for his contribution, pays such money and also his share of all profits made. Other forms include mergers and acquisition. No need to go into legal terms and details. The important thing is that what one business cannot afford to do alone, it can now do it by joining others to do it jointly.

Macro-Economic Management (The Role of Government)

Going by the government's position as a bedrock in the marking of a viable economy, the government of the Eastern states have a vital role to play.

1. It will entail the setting up of a commission vested with purely technical, commercial and management consultancy aids. Through this commission, the government will not only give advisory and enlightenment services to the public but also receive reports of public complaints and the extent of the implementation of government's programmes. This is very necessary since a high percentage of these businessmen are uneducated and need to be counseled through the commission about the importance of going public (P.L.C.) and forming co-operative societies in order to protect the life of growing business and other related issues.

2. Other services of the commission will include the mapping out of industrial estates and commercial cities out of the already existing rural favourable climate. By the order, the commission should ensure that there is strict specialization and specification of trade and absolute decentralization in mapping of the said industrial estates and commercial cities according to geographical spread. This will enhance a uniform development and easy identification.

3. Knowing that mobility stands as a unique factor in the making of an economy, the government should encourage this vision through provision of feeder roads network, communication and other related facilities.

4. And finally, since it will not be so convenient for a man who has his firm in the East, to transverse lands to such far away Apapa or Tin-can Island wharfs for the clearing or the forwarding of either his raw-materials or his finished products, government should endeavor to embark on the ever procrastinated port development of the Oguta Lake and Onitsha end of the River Niger for shuttle

marine services. In addition is the internationaliza-tion of Airports in the heart of Igbo land to serve that catchment area. These and lots more, when implemented, will make our dreamed industrial-ised A.D. 2033 a reality.

Towards the Implementation of This Laudable Vision

1. This project is the brain child of Africa Economic Empowerment initiative, AEEI, whose pellucid vision is to create 500,000 jobs through Micro, Small, and Medium Enterprises (MSME) develop-ment, training and empowerment for youths in Africa within 10 years.

2. As it concerns this immediate project, AEEI intends to redirect the business and investment culture of the Igbos, to achieve a safe anchor base for their labours in the South East, Nigeria.

3. AEEI will propose South East Industrial Mobi-lization Project—SEIMP to South East Governors Forum and Ohaneze Ndigbo for partnership.

4. Propose a SEIMP Commission to be headed by a Commissioner. AEEI and SEIMP will partner for

effective project implementation and monitoring.

5. The Commission/AEEI will partner with GIL Consults for all trainings necessary for beneficiaries' participation in the industrial project through Enterprise Development. They will also handle all support services such as company promotion or formation, acceleration and incubation to assist start-up businesses and factories.

6. Then comes the inaugural lecture for the formal launching of SOUTHEAST INDUSTRIAL MOBILISATION PROJECT before the stakeholders and all Nigerians.

7. SEIMP also known as 'Vision 2033' has a ten-year implementation schedule to deliver South-East industrialization through short term, medium term, and long-term plans.

8. In view of this, online registration of membership has commenced. To benefit from this project and to receive regular updates, visit **http://www.aeeiafrica.org/membership-application-guide/** to register with AEEI.